# THE LITTLE ZOO

The most interesting and fun facts about wild exotic animals with beautiful illustrations.

# ELEPHANT

There are two types of elephant, the Asian elephant, and the African elephant. African elephants are larger than Asian elephants and have larger ears. Elephants are the largest land-living mammal in the world.

Both female and male African elephants have tusks but only the male Asian elephants have tusks. They use their tusks for digging and finding food.

Female elephants are called cows. They start to have calves when they are about 12 years old and they are pregnant for 22 months.

An elephant can use its tusks to dig for ground water. An adult elephant needs to drink around 55 gals (210 L) of water a day, and eat 300-600 lbs (135-272 kg).

Elephants have large, thin ears that are made up of a complex network of blood vessels which help regulate their temperature. Blood is circulated through their ears to cool them down in hot climates.

The elephant's trunk is able to sense the size, shape, and temperature of an object. An elephant uses its trunk to lift food and suck up water then pour it into its mouth.

An elephant's trunk can grow to be about 6.5 ft (2 m) long and can weigh up to 308 lbs (140 kg). Elephants can swim – they use their trunk to breathe like a snorkel in deep water.

Elephants are herbivores and can spend up to 16 hours a day collecting leaves, twigs, bamboo, and roots.

Scientists discovered that elephants sing. They use an ultrasound rumble too low for humans to hear to keep the heard together and to find mates. Adult elephants eat 300-600 lbs (135-272 kg) of food every day.

Elephants sleep about 2 hours per day. The average lifespan for an elephant is 60-70 years.

# KANGAROO

Kangaroos are marsupials - animals that have a pouch, they carry their young in their pouch. They are the largest marsupials on the planet.

They live mostly in Australia, but some sub-species of kangaroo can also be found in Papua New Guinea and Tasmania. Kangaroos are herbivores - animals that don't eat meat, they mostly eat grass, shoots, and shrubs.

A baby kangaroo is called a joey. When a joey is born it is only about 1 inch (2.5 cm) long. A joey will stay in their mom's pouch for at least 4 months. They can hop in and out of their mother's pouch until they are about 10 months old. After 10 months they leave their mom's pouch for good. Here is a fun fact about kangaroos…they cannot walk backwards! The average lifespan of a kangaroo is 23 years.

Kangaroos can be 6 ft -10 ft (1.8 - 3 m) tall. Kangaroos can jump 25 ft (7.6 m) in a single leap! These animals use their tails to help balance while jumping. Kangaroos can also run fast. They can reach speeds of 35 miles (56 km) per hour. When a kangaroo feels threatened it will pound the ground with its feet and kick. Kangaroos can swim.

Kangaroos can hop around quickly on two legs or walk around slowly on all four. Young kangaroos (joeys) will sometimes jump head first into their mother's pouch when frightened. Kangaroos have excellent hearing, and like some other animals are able to move their ears in different directions without moving the rest of their head. Kangaroos are social animals which stay in groups of at least 3 or 4 individuals. Some groups can comprise of as many as 100 individuals.

There are more kangaroos than humans in Australia. They are the national symbol of Australia and appear on postage stamps, coins, and airplanes.

# CAMEL

There are two species of true camel. The dromedary is a single-humped camel that lives in the Middle East and the Horn of Africa area. The Bactrian is a two-humped camel that lives in areas of Central Asia.

There are four camel-like mammals that live in South America, llama and alpaca are called "New World camels", while guanaco and vicuna are called "South American camels".

Camels have been domesticated by humans for thousands of years. Used mostly for transport or to carry heavy loads, they also provide a source of milk, meat, and hair/wool.

Camels live on average for 40 to 50 years. They are 3.3 ft (1.8 m) at shoulder level and 6.5 ft (2.2 m) at the hump. They are capable of running as fast as 40 mph (65 km/h) for a short period of time and can maintain a speed of around 25 mph (40 km/h).

Dromedary camels weigh 660 to 1320 lbs (300 to 600 kg) and Bactrian camels weigh 660 to 2.200 lbs (300 to 1000 kg).

Camels do not actually hold liquid water in their humps. The humps contain fatty tissue reserves, which can be converted to water or energy when required. They can survive up to six months without food or water by using up these fatty stores.

Camels are well suited to the hot sandy deserts they roam in. Their thick coat insulates them from heat and also lightens during summer to help reflect heat.

A camel's long legs help its body to be high from the hot desert surface and a pad of thick tissue called a pedestal raises the body slightly when the camel sits so cool air can pass underneath.

A large camel can drink around 30 gallons (113 liters) in just 13 minutes, making them able to rehydrate faster than any other mammal.

Long eyelashes, ear hair, and closable nostrils keep sand from affecting the camel, while their wide feet help them move without sinking into the sand.

# TIGER

Tigers live on the continent of Asia in grasslands, forest, and swamps. As the largest member of the cat family, tigers are strong, powerful and one of nature's most feared predators. Their beautiful orange and black striped coats provide camouflage when hunting prey at night when they can reach speeds of 40 mph (65 km/h).

They can weight between 250-700 pounds (113-317 kg), and be 6–11 feet (1.8-3.4 m) long with a 3 foot (90 cm) long tail. Tigers can run up to 40 mph (65 km/h) and jump 16 feet (5 m) high.

They are the 3rd largest land carnivore in the world. Polar Bears are first and Brown Bears are second. Tigers are powerful apex predators that are at the top of the food chain and capable of killing animals over twice their size. They are nocturnal hunters and will travel many miles to prey on a variety of animals including deer, buffalo, and wild boar; native ungulates are the favorite. A tigers roar can be heard over 2 miles (3.2 km) away.

Tigers are solitary, living alone in scent-marked territories that vary in size depending on the availability of prey. If there is plenty of prey available, the area can support more tigers, so territories will be smaller and tiger numbers higher. A tiger can eat up 60 pounds (27 kg) of meat but usually, they eat less.

Unlike other cats, tigers are good swimmers and often cool off in lakes and streams during the heat of the day. They can swim up to 4 miles (6.5 km).

Not only are tigers fur stripped but their skin is stripped too! A tiger retracts their claws when walking, they do not leave claw prints in their footprints.

They live alone and scent-mark their territories. A male tiger guards his territory against other males but must offer access to females for potential mating. A male's territory will always be larger than a female's and may overlap with the territories of one to seven females.

Tigers can live up to 26 years in captivity and 10-15 years in the wild. There are more tigers living in captivity than there are in the wild. The only predator to a tiger is a human. A major threat to tigers is a loss of habitat and hunting.

# FLAMINGO

Flamingos are a type of wading bird that live in areas of large shallow lakes, lagoons, mangrove swamps, tidal flats, and sandy islands. There are six species of flamingo in the world. Two are found in the Old World and four species live in the New World - Americas.

The most widespread flamingo is the Greater flamingo found in areas of Africa, Southern Europe and South, Southwest Asia. The Lesser flamingo is the most numerous and lives in the Great Rift Valley of Africa through to Northwest India.

The Greater flamingo is the largest species, at up to 5 ft (1.5 m) tall and weighing up to 3.5 kg (8 lbs). The Lesser flamingo is just 3 ft (90 cm) tall, weighing 5.5 lbs (2.5 kg). In the wild flamingos live 20 - 30 years and sometimes over 50 years in captivity.

Flamingo legs can be longer than their entire body. The backward bending "knee" of a flamingo's leg is actually its ankle, the knee is out of sight further up the leg. Quite often flamingos will stand on one leg, with the other tucked under the body. It's not fully understood why they do this but it is believed to conserve body heat.

The flamingo is a filter-feeder, holding its curved beak upside down in the water it sucks in the muddy water and pushes the mud and silt out the side while tiny hair-like filters along the beak called lamellae sieve food from the water.

The pink to reddish color of a flamingo's feathers comes from carotenoids (the pigment that also makes carrots orange) in their diet of plankton, brine shrimp, and blue-green algae.

Flamingos are social birds, they live in colonies of sometimes thousands, this helps in avoiding predators, maximizing food intake, and is better for nesting. Flamingo colonies split into breeding groups of up to 50 birds, who then perform a synchronized ritual 'dance' whereby they stand together stretching their necks upwards, uttering calls while waving their heads and then flapping their wings.

# PARROT

Parrots can reach 4 to 40 inches (10 to 100 cm) in length, depending on the species. Smallest species of parrot, buff-faced pygmy parrot, is only 3 inches (7.5 cm) long and weighs 0.4 ounces (11 g).

All parrots are brightly colored, have curved beaks and strong legs that end with four toes. Two toes are positioned forward and two backward. The arrangement of toes and sharp claws facilitate life on the trees and ensure a firm grip when parrots rest on the branches.

Parrots are the only birds that are able to pick food with their feet and bring it to the mouth. Parrots are able to imitate human voice, but only domesticated parrots have this unusual habit.

Parrots are extremely intelligent animals. African grey parrot, named Alex, managed to learn to count to 6, answer the questions, recognize 7 colors and identify 35 different objects.

Parrots are omnivores (they eat other animals and plants). Their diet consists of seed, nuts, fruit, flowers, and insects.

Parrots live in large groups called flocks that usually consist of 20 to 30 animals. They produce loud screeching noise and use body language for communication. Main predators of parrots are snakes, birds of prey, monkeys, and humans. Parrots build nests in the tree holes, cavities in the cliffs, termite mounds or use ground tunnels.

Most species of parrots are monogamous (one pair creates a bond that lasts forever). Smaller species of parrots can survive up to 10 years in the captivity while larger species have a lifespan of nearly 80 years.

# IGUANA

Iguana is a type of large lizards. It can be found in Mexico, Central America, Brazil and on Caribbean Islands. Different species live in different habitats. Some iguanas prefer life in tropical rainforests, some in the water, while others enjoy life in desert conditions. Iguana can vary in size depending on the species. On average, they are usually 6 to 6.5 feet (1.8 - 2 m) long, weight 11 pounds (5 kg). Iguanas are the largest lizards in America.

Iguana has strong jaws with sharp teeth. They have very long and sharp tail that is usually half of the body size.

The tail is used mainly for defense (iguana can punch its enemy with tail). In the case of danger, the iguana can detach a part of its tail to ensure fast escape from a predator. Just like in other lizards, iguana's "broken" tail will soon heal and reach its previous size.

Green iguana has a third eye. This retina-like structure is located on the top of the head and it is connected with a pineal gland in the brain. Although it does not produce images like a regular eye, it reacts to the changes in light and it is used for detection of predators above the head.

Some of the worst enemies of iguana are predatory birds. Iguana often freezes on the sound of hawk's whistle and unfortunately becomes even easier prey for catching. Although they are stable and safe on trees, they may occasionally fall down. The iguana can survive fall from the height of 40 to 50 feet (12 to 15 m) without injuries.

Iguana is a herbivore (plant-eater). It likes to eat fruit, leaves, and flowers. They are often found near the water. They are known as excellent swimmers.

# SHARK

The shark is the largest fish in the sea.

A shark does not have a single bone in it body, instead, it has a skeleton made up of cartilage. Cartilage is a tough material, like the material that shapes your ear.

Sharks are strong, healthy creatures. No other living thing can take better care of itself than a shark can. Sharks never get cancer, so their cartilage is being studied with the hope of developing anti-cancer drugs.

Most sharks live for about 25 years, while some can live to be a 100 years too. Most kinds of sharks can swim up to 20-40 miles (30-65 km) per hour. Not all species of sharks are required to be in continuous motion to breathe, however a shark's body is heavier than the sea, so if it stops moving it will sink. Sharks do not sleep in the same way as humans. Even if they seem to be sleeping they are not, instead they are just resting.

A shark's teeth are usually replaced every eight days. Some species of sharks shed about 30,000 teeth in their lifetime. When a shark loses a tooth, one replaces it. A Whale Shark has more than 4,000 teeth, but each is less than 1/8 inch (3 mm) long.

Sharks have very good senses. Sometimes a shark is called "a swimming nose", for its great sense of smell. Sharks can easily detect prey that is in the sand, as well as at night.

A shark also has a remarkable sensitivity to vibrations in the water. It can feel the movements made by other animals that are hundreds of feet away. They can hear sounds from thousands of feet away. Sharks can tell the direction from where the sound is coming from, too.

One good meal is enough to satisfy a shark's hunger. The meal can last a shark for a long period because it uses very little energy to swim. Some sharks hold food in their stomachs without it being digested. If they eat a big meal, it can last three or more months.

# POLAR BEAR

Polar bears are found in the frozen wilds of the Arctic, in Canada, Alaska (US), Greenland, Russia, and Norway.

Adult polar bears can measure over 6.5 ft (2.5 m) long and weigh around 1500 lb (680 kg). Their huge size and weight make them the largest living carnivores (meat eaters) on Earth!

Polar bears are well adapted to survive in one of the harshest environments on our planet. As well as their thick fur, they have a layer of fat, called blubber, that insulates (protects) their bodies from the frosty air and near-freezing water. Polar bears also have black skin under their glistening coat, which helps them soak up the Sun's rays and keep warm.

These magnificent mammals have an incredible sense of smell which they use to track their favorite grub, seals. In fact, their sense of smell is so good, they can sniff out prey from up to 10 miles (16 km) away!

Despite their size and bulk, polar bears are excellent swimmers and have been spotted in waters over 100 km offshore. They can comfortably swim at around 6 miles/h (10 km/h) using their slightly webbed, 11 inches (30 cm) wide paws like paddles in the water.

Although good swimmers, polar bears aren't quick enough to reliably catch seals in open water. Instead, they depend on the ice as a hunting platform. They wait near seal breathing holes or at the ice's edge for a seal to surface. They then snatch it from the sea and…gulp!

At birth, the cubs are only around 11 inches (30 cm) long and weigh around 1 lb (0.5 kg) – that's about the same as a guinea pig! Polar bears have black skin and although their fur appears white, it is actually transparent.

Female polar bears usually only weigh about half as much as males. Polar bears have black skin and although their fur appears white, it is actually transparent. Female polar bears usually only weigh about half as much as males.

# LEOPARD

Most leopards are light colored and have dark spots on their fur. These spots are called "rosettes" because their shape is similar to that of a rose. There are also black leopards, too, whose spots are hard to see because their fur is so dark.

Leopards can be found in various places around the world – they live in Sub-Saharan Africa, northeast Africa, Central Asia, India, and China.

Leopards are fast felines and can run at up to 36 miles/h (58 km/h). They're super springy, too, and can leap 20 ft (6 m) forward through the air!

Leopards are very solitary and spend most of their time alone. They each have their own territory, and leave scratches on trees, urine scent marks and poop to warn other leopards to stay away! Males and females will cross territories, but only to mate.

These big cats eat bugs, fish, antelope, monkeys, rodents, deer…in fact, pretty much any prey that is available!

Leopards are skilled climbers and like to rest in the branches of trees during the day. They are strong beasts, too, and can carry their heavy prey up into the trees so that pesky scavengers, such as hyenas, don't steal their meal!

Nocturnal animals, leopards are active at night when they venture out in search for food. They spend their days mostly resting, camouflaged in the trees or hiding in caves.

When a leopard spots a potential meal, it approaches with legs bent and head low, so as not to be seen. It then stalks its prey carefully and quietly, until its five to ten meters within range. Then…pounce! The leopard dashes forward and takes down its victim with a bite to the throat or neck. Small prey, such as small birds or mice, will receive a fatal blow from the felines paw. Ouch!

Leopards communicate with each other through distinctive calls. For instance, when one male wants to make another aware of his presence, he'll make a hoarse, raspy cough. They also growl when angry and, like domestic cats, purr when happy and relaxed. Cute, eh?

# CROCODILE

A crocodile is a large amphibious reptile. It lives mostly in large tropical rivers, where it is an ambush predator. One species, the Australian saltie, also travels in coastal salt water. This crocodile is the largest species of crocodile and can grow to be 7-15 feet (2-4.5 m) and weight up to 2600 lb (1200 kg).

In very dry climates, crocodiles may sleep until the dry season ends.

Crocodiles are reptiles that live mostly in large tropical rivers. Like other reptiles, the crocodile is a cold-blooded animal.

The physical characteristics of crocodiles make them good predators. They are known for their ability to hide in plain sight and ambush their prey.

Crocodiles are fast over short distances both on land and in the water as well. This helps in their predatory abilities. They have sharp teeth and have the strongest bite of any animal in the world.

Even though the crocodile has a strong bite, the muscles that open their jaws are not that powerful and a reasonably strong human could hold their jaw closed with their bare hands.

Crocodiles can survive for a long time without food. When they do eat, the crocodile has a variety of fish, birds and other animals. Crocodiles release heat through their mouths rather than through sweat glands.

American crocodiles are much less aggressive than the Nile and Australian crocodiles and are much shyer and reclusive.

The greatest threats to crocodiles are a loss of their habitat because of human development, illegal killing by poachers, and roadkill.

## PANDA

Pandas are much bigger than you think. An adult panda weight more than 100 lbs (45 kg), and can be about 1.5 meters (5 feet) long!

Giant pandas can't stand and do kung fu moves like Po in Kungfu Panda. But they are good tree climbers. They can climb trees from 7 months old. Giant pandas are bears, and like other bears, they can swim.

Pandas are born looking like baby badgers: fur-less, pink, and blind. The iconic black and white color come later, after about three weeks. Not all giant pandas are black and white! A few are brown and white, but these are very rare.

As about, all a panda does all day is eating and sleeping, you are best to get up early for a visit to a panda park, so you see them when they are active.

One reason for pandas being rare is that breeding is not high on their list of priorities. And with only a one-day window a year for a female to conceive naturally, it is hardly surprising that pandas are an endangered species.

Giant pandas' diets are 99% bamboo. Their favorite food is bamboo shoots. A 100 lbs (45 kg) adult (and pandas can reach 150 kg in captivity) spends as long as 14 hours eating. And it can eat 26 to 85 lbs (12 to 38 kg) of bamboo a day.

Pandas can poop as much as 28 kg/day. Panda's poop points in their direction of travel, so they can be easily tracked in the wild. Unfortunately, historically this led to them being more endangered, but now it aids researchers. Since giant predators like sabre-tooth tigers are no longer around, pandas didn't need to be as fast and turned into vegetarian specialists to avoid becoming extinct themselves.

Although they still have sharp teeth and the digestive tract of carnivores, they don't have the energy to chase anything, so their prey would virtually have to land in their lap, or be injured and too slow to escape. Pandas are usually born in August because the panda's mating months are March to May and gestation is 3 to 5 months.

# WOLF

Wolves are excellent hunters and have been found to be living in more places in the world than any other mammal except humans. The wolf is the ancestor of all breeds of domestic dog. It is part of a group of animals called the wild dogs which also includes the dingo and the coyote.

Most wolves weigh about 88 lbs (40 kg) but the heaviest wolf ever recorded weighed over 175 lbs (80 kg)! Adult wolves have large feet. A fully grown wolf would have a paw print nearly 5 inches (13 cm) long and 4 inches (10 cm) wide.

Wolves live and hunt in groups called a pack. A pack can range from two wolves to as many as 20 wolves depending on such factors as habitat and food supply. Most packs have one breeding pair of wolves, called the alpha pair, who leads the hunt. Wolf pups are born deaf and blind while weighing around 1 lb (0.5 kg). It takes about 8 months before they are old enough to actively join in wolf pack hunts.

Wolves in the Arctic have to travel much longer distances than wolves in the forest to find food and will sometimes go for several days without eating.

When hunting alone, the wolf catches small animals such as squirrels, hares, chipmunks, raccoons or rabbits. However, a pack of wolves can hunt very large animals like moose, caribou, and yaks.

When the pack kills an animal, the alpha pair always eats first. As food supply is often irregular for wolves, they will eat up to 1/5th of their own body weight at a time to make up for days of missed food.

Wolves have two layers of fur, an undercoat, and a top coat, which allow them to survive in temperatures as low as minus 40 degrees Celsius! In warmer weather, they flatten their fur to keep cool.

A wolf can run at a speed of 40 miles/h (65 km/h) during a chase. Wolves have long legs and spend most of their time trotting at a speed of 7.5-10 miles/h (12-16 km/h). They can keep up a reasonable pace for hours and have been known to cover distances of 55 miles/h (90 km) in one night.

# KOALA

Koalas are found in the eucalyptus forests of eastern Australia. They have grey fur with a cream-colored chest, and strongly clawed feet, perfect for living in the branches of trees!

Cuddly critters, koalas measure about 25 to 35 inches (60 to 85 cm) long and weigh about 30 lbs (14 kg). These awesome animals aren't bears – they are marsupials. A group of mammals, most marsupials have pouches where their newborns develop. When an infant koala – called a joey – is born, it immediately climbs up to its mother's pouch. Blind and earless, a joey uses its strong sense of touch and smell, as well as natural instinct, to find its way.

A joey grows and develops in the pouch for about six months. Once strong enough, the youngster rides around on its mother's back for a further six months, only using the pouch to feed.

Koalas grow up to become big eaters, shifting up to one kg of eucalyptus leaves in a day! They are fussy, too, and will select the most nutritious and tastiest leaves from the trees where they live.

These magnificent mammals get their name from an Aboriginal* term meaning, 'no drink'. It's believed this is because koalas get almost all their moisture from the leaves they eat, and rarely drink water.

But check this out – eucalyptus leaves are super tough and poisonous! Luckily for koalas, they have a long digestive organ called a cecum which allows them to break down the leaves unharmed.

Enjoy having a snooze? Well so do our furry friends! Koalas don't have much energy and, when not feasting on leaves, they spend their time dozing in the branches. Believe it or not, they can sleep for up to 18 hours a day!

Although these beautiful creatures are protected by law, and not classed as an endangered species, their habitat is under threat. Sadly, around 80% of koala habitat has been lost to human homes, drought and forest fires.

Please visit my author's page on Amazon.com to find out more cool books for children.